school - Schule	2
travel - Reise	5
transport - Transport	8
city - Stadt	10
landscape - Landschaft	14
restaurant - Restaurant	17
supermarket - Supermarkt	20
drinks - Getränke	22
food - Essen	23
farm - Bauernhof	27
house - Haus	31
living room - Wohnzimmer	33
kitchen - Küche	35
bathroom - Badezimmer	38
child's room - Kinderzimmer	42
clothing - Kleidung	44
office - Büro	49
economy - Wirtschaft	51
occupations - Berufe	53
tools - Werkzeuge	56
musical instruments - Musikinstrumente	57
zoo - Zoo	59
sports - Sport	62
activities - Aktivitäten	63
family - Familie	67
body - Körper	68
hospital - Krankenhaus	72
emergency - Notfall	76
Earth - Erde	77
clock - Uhr	79
week - Woche	80
year - Jahr	81
shapes - Formen	83
colours - Farben	84
opposites - Gegenteile	85
numbers - Zahlen	88
languages - Sprachen	90
who / what / how - wer / was / wie	91
where - wo	92

Impressum
Verlag: BABADADA GmbH, Nedderfeld 112 , 22529 Hamburg
Geschäftsführer / Verlagsleitung: Harald Hof
Druck: Books on Demand GmbH, In de Tarpen 42, 22848 Norderstedt

Imprint
Publisher: BABADADA GmbH, Nedderfeld 112 , 22529 Hamburg, Germany
Managing Director / Publishing direction: Harald Hof
Print: Books on Demand GmbH, In de Tarpen 42, 22848 Norderstedt

school

Schule

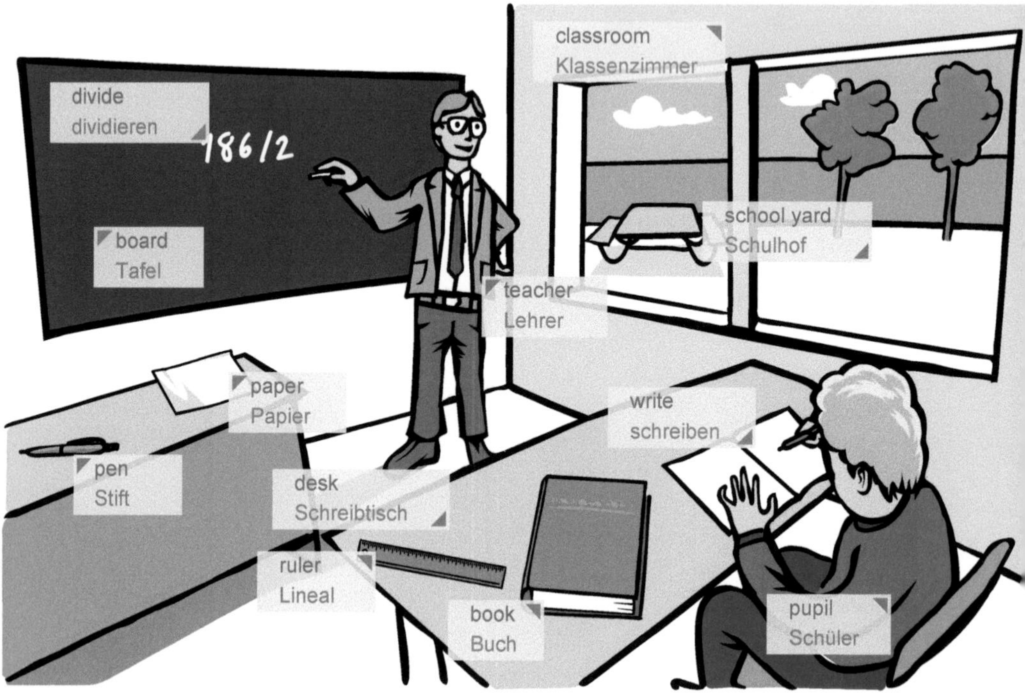
classroom
Klassenzimmer
divide
dividieren
186/2
board
Tafel
school yard
Schulhof
teacher
Lehrer
paper
Papier
write
schreiben
pen
Stift
desk
Schreibtisch
ruler
Lineal
book
Buch
pupil
Schüler

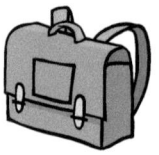

satchel

Ranzen

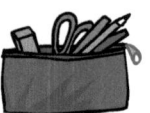

pencil case

Federmappe

pencil

Bleistift

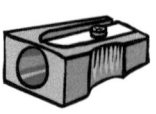

pencil sharpener

Bleistiftanspitzer

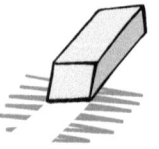

rubber

Radiergummi

drawing pad

Zeichenblock

drawing

Zeichnung

paintbrush

Pinsel

paint box

Malkasten

scissors

Schere

glue

Klebstoff

exercise book

Übungsheft

homework

Hausaufgabe

number

Zahl

add

addieren

subtract

subtrahieren

multiply

multiplizieren

calculate

rechnen

letter

Buchstabe

alphabet

Alphabet

word

Wort

text

Text

read

lesen

chalk

Kreide

lesson

Stunde

register

Klassenbuch

exam

Prüfung

certificate

Zeugnis

school uniform

Schuluniform

education

Ausbildung

encyclopedia

Lexikon

university

Universität

microscope

Mikroskop

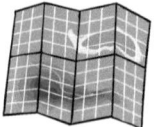

map

Karte

waste-paper basket

Papierkorb

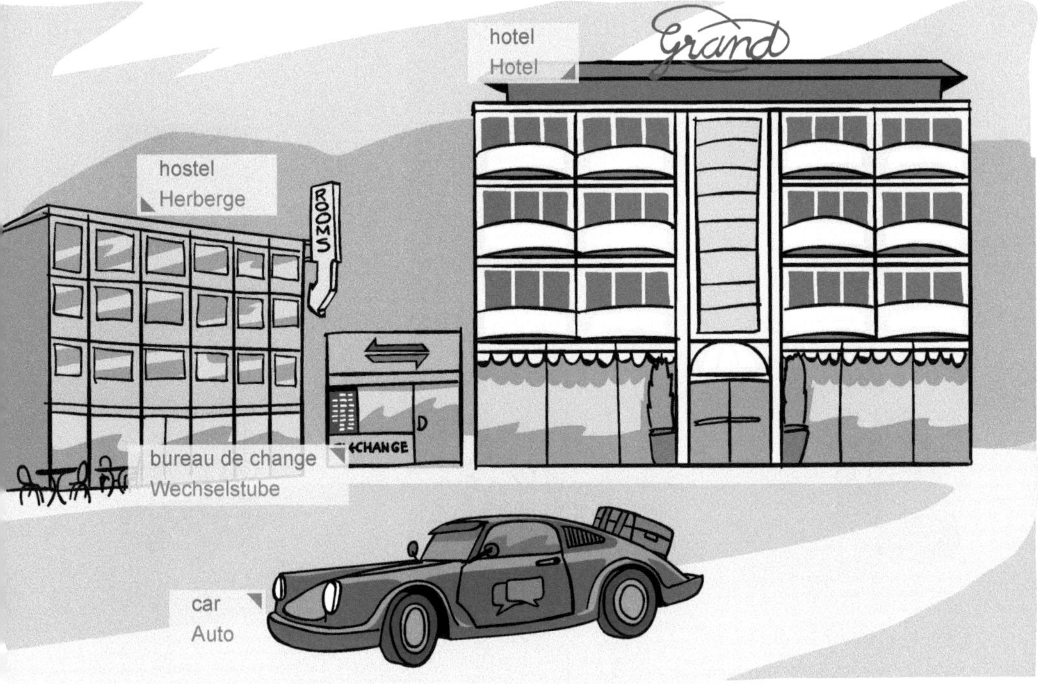

hotel
Hotel
Grand
hostel
Herberge
ROOMS
CHANGE
bureau de change
Wechselstube
car
Auto

language
Sprache

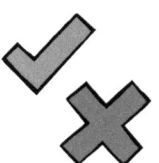

yes / no
ja / nein

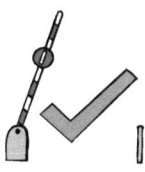

Okay
Okay

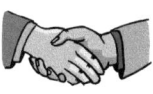

hello
Hallo

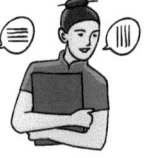

translator
Übersetzer

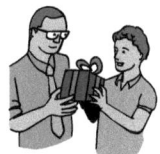

Thank you
Danke

how much is...?

Was kostet...?

I do not understand

Ich verstehe nicht

problem

Problem

Good evening!

Guten Abend!

Good morning!

Guten Morgen!

Good night!

Gute Nacht!

bye bye

Auf Wiedersehen

direction

Richtung

luggage

Gepäck

bag

Tasche

backpack

Rucksack

guest

Gast

room

Zimmer

sleeping bag

Schlafsack

tent

Zelt

travel - Reise

tourist information

Touristeninformation

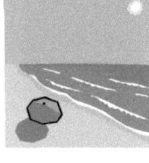

beach

Strand

credit card

Kreditkarte

breakfast

Frühstück

lunch

Mittagessen

dinner

Abendessen

ticket

Fahrkarte

lift

Fahrstuhl

stamp

Briefmarke

border

Grenze

customs

Zoll

embassy

Botschaft

visa

Visum

passport

Pass

transport
Transport

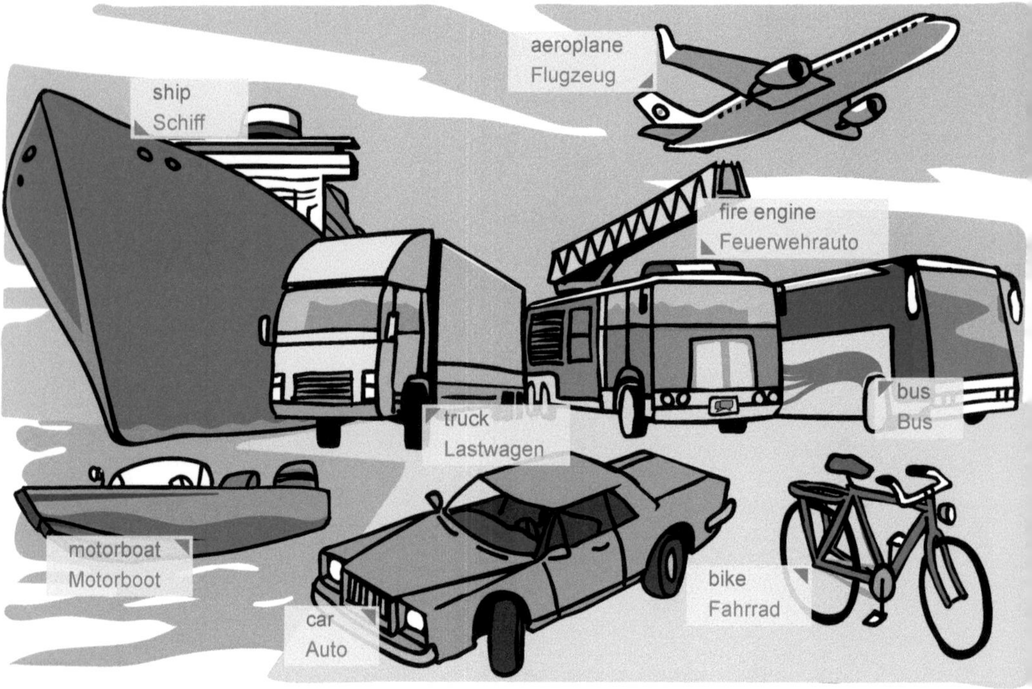

aeroplane
Flugzeug
ship
Schiff
fire engine
Feuerwehrauto
bus
Bus
truck
Lastwagen
motorboat
Motorboot
bike
Fahrrad
car
Auto

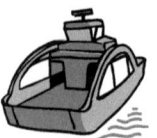

ferry

Fähre

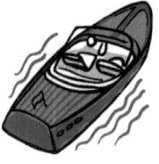

boat

Boot

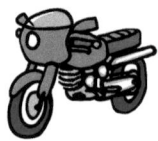

motorbike

Motorrad

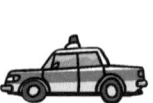

police car

Polizeiauto

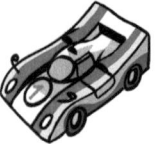

racing car

Rennauto

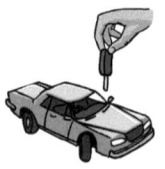

rental car

Mietwagen

car sharing

Carsharing

breakdown truck

Abschleppwagen

refuse truck

Müllauto

motor

Motor

fuel

Kraftstoff

petrol station

Tankstelle

traffic sign

Verkehrsschild

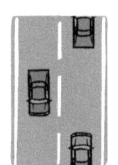

traffic

Verkehr

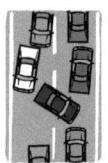

traffic jam

Stau

car park

Parkplatz

train station

Bahnhof

tracks

Schienen

train

Zug

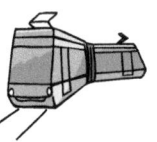

tram

Straßenbahn

carriage

Wagon

helicopter

Helikopter

airport

Flughafen

tower

Tower

passenger

Passagier

container

Container

carton

Karton

cart

Karren

basket

Korb

take off / land

starten / landen

city

Stadt

village

Dorf

city centre

Stadtzentrum

house

Haus

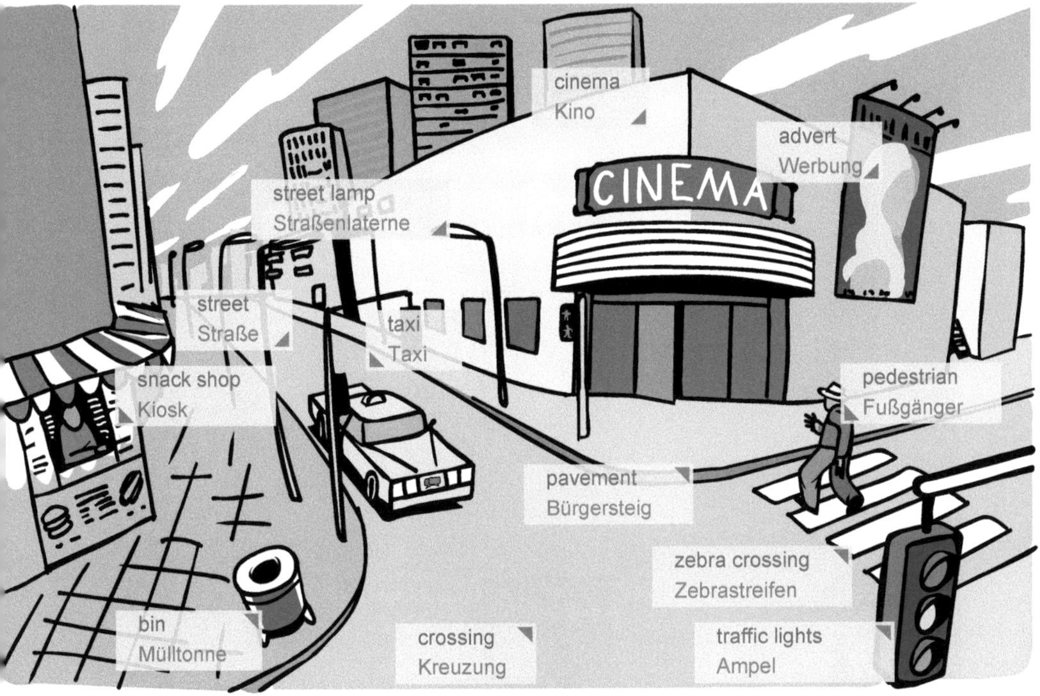

cinema
Kino

advert
Werbung

street lamp
Straßenlaterne

CINEMA

street
Straße

taxi
Taxi

snack shop
Kiosk

pedestrian
Fußgänger

pavement
Bürgersteig

zebra crossing
Zebrastreifen

bin
Mülltonne

crossing
Kreuzung

traffic lights
Ampel

hut
Hütte

flat
Wohnung

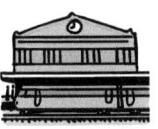

train station
Bahnhof

town hall
Rathaus

museum
Museum

school
Schule

university

Universität

bank

Bank

hospital

Krankenhaus

hotel

Hotel

pharmacy

Apotheke

office

Büro

book shop

Buchhandlung

shop

Geschäft

florist's

Blumenladen

supermarket

Supermarkt

market

Markt

department store

Kaufhaus

fishmonger's

Fischhändler

shopping centre

Einkaufszentrum

harbour

Hafen

city - Stadt

park

Park

bench

Bank

bridge

Brücke

stairs

Treppe

underground

U-Bahn

tunnel

Tunnel

bus stop

Bushaltestelle

bar

Bar

restaurant

Restaurant

postbox

Briefkasten

street sign

Straßenschild

parking meter

Parkuhr

zoo

Zoo

swimming pool

Badeanstalt

mosque

Moschee

farm
Bauernhof

pollution
Umweltverschmutzung

graveyard
Friedhof

church
Kirche

playground
Spielplatz

temple
Tempel

landscape
Landschaft

signpost
Wegweiser

way
Weg

meadow
Wiese

stone
Stein

hiker
Wanderer

tree
Baum

river
Fluss

grass
Gras

flower
Blume

valley

Tal

hill

Berg

lake

See

forest

Wald

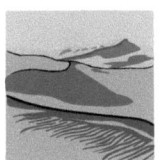

desert

Wüste

volcano

Vulkan

castle

Schloss

rainbow

Regenbogen

mushroom

Pilz

palm tree

Palme

mosquito

Moskito

fly

Fliege

ant

Ameise

bee

Biene

spider

Spinne

beetle

Käfer

frog

Frosch

squirrel

Eichhörnchen

hedgehog

Igel

hare

Hase

owl

Eule

bird

Vogel

swan

Schwan

boar

Wildschwein

deer

Hirsch

moose

Elch

dam

Staudamm

wind turbine

Windrad

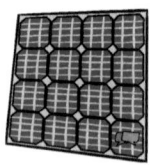

solar panel

Solarmodul

climate

Klima

landscape - Landschaft

restaurant
Restaurant

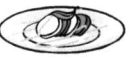

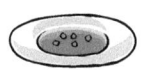

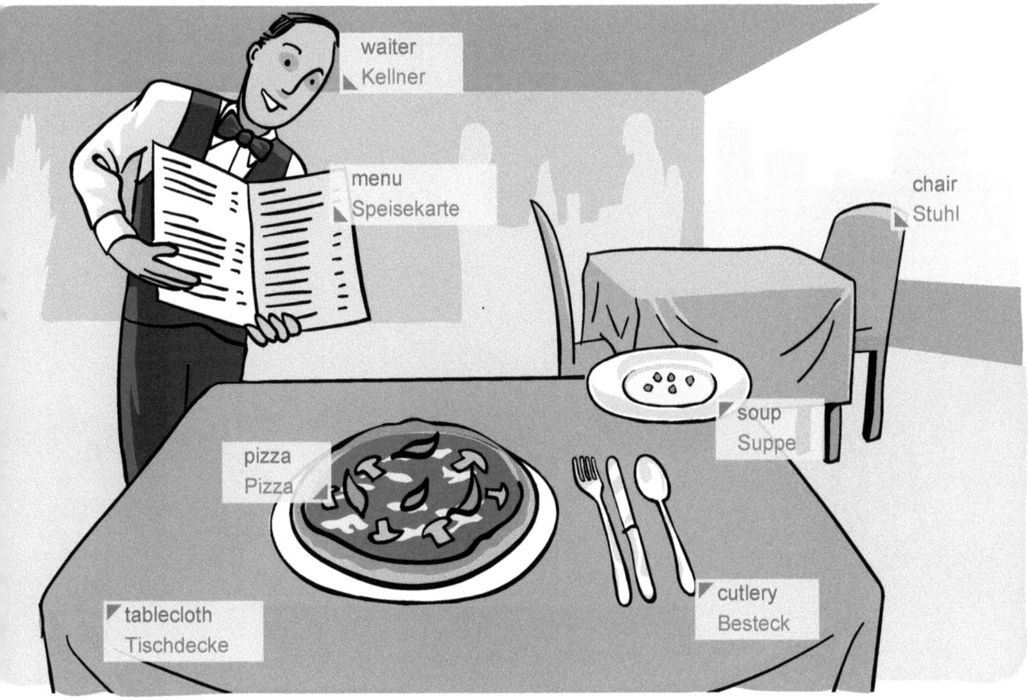
waiter
Kellner
menu
Speisekarte
chair
Stuhl
soup
Suppe
pizza
Pizza
cutlery
Besteck
tablecloth
Tischdecke

starter

Vorspeise

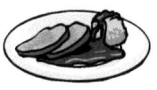

main course

Hauptgericht

dessert

Nachspeise

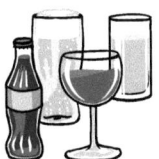

drinks

Getränke

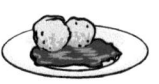

food

Essen

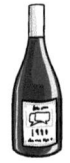

bottle

Flasche

fast food

Fastfood

street food

Streetfood

teapot

Teekanne

sugar bowl

Zuckerdose

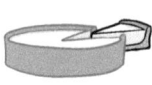

portion

Portion

espresso machine

Espressomaschine

high chair

Hochstuhl

bill

Rechnung

tray

Tablett

knife

Messer

fork

Gabel

spoon

Löffel

teaspoon

Teelöffel

serviette

Serviette

glass

Glas

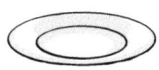

plate

Teller

soup plate

Suppenteller

saucer

Untertasse

sauce

Sauce

salt pot

Salzstreuer

pepper mill

Pfeffermühle

vinegar

Essig

oil

Öl

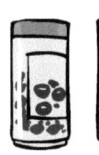

spices

Gewürze

ketchup

Ketchup

mustard

Senf

mayonnaise

Mayonnaise

supermarket
Supermarkt

special offer
Angebot
FOR
customer
Kunde
dairy
Milchprodukte
fruit
Obst
trolley
Einkaufswagen

BUTCHERS

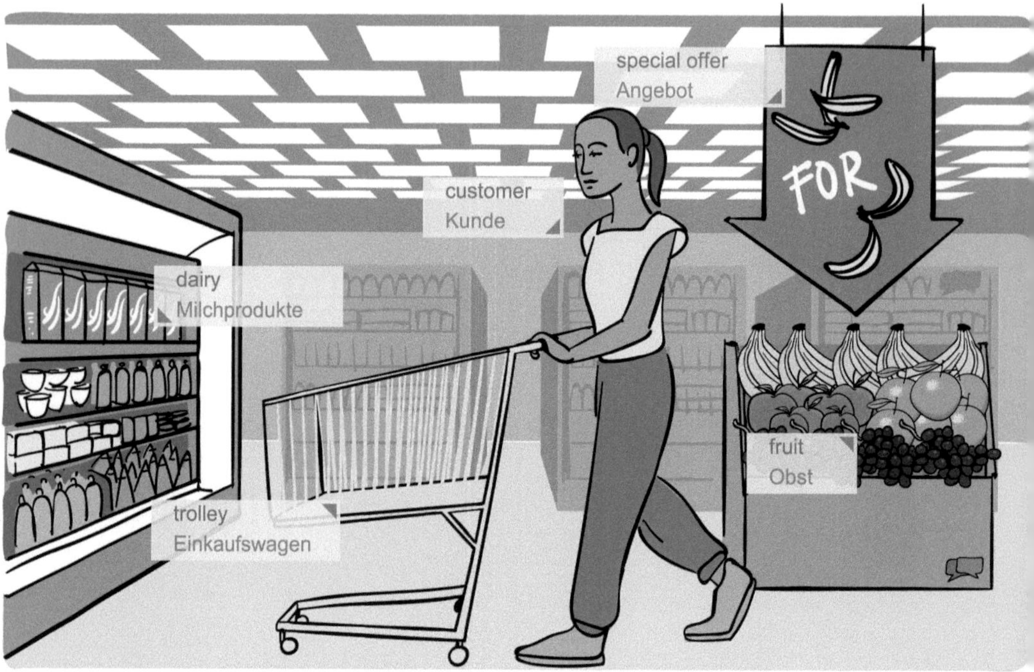

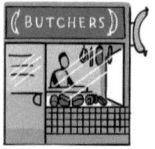

butcher´s

Schlachterei

BAKERY

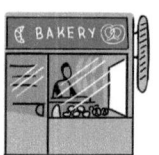

baker´s

Bäckerei

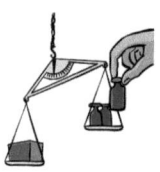

weigh

wiegen

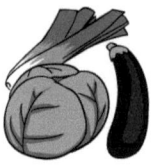

vegetables

Gemüse

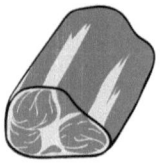

meat

Fleisch

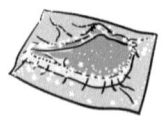

frozen food

Tiefkühlkost

cold meat

Aufschnitt

tinned food

Konserven

washing powder

Waschmittel

sweets

Süßigkeiten

household products

Haushaltsartikel

cleaning products

Reinigungsmittel

salesperson

Verkäuferin

till

Kasse

cashier

Kassierer

shopping list

Einkaufsliste

opening hours

Öffnungszeiten

wallet

Brieftasche

credit card

Kreditkarte

bag

Tasche

plastic bag

Plastiktüte

water	juice	milk
Wasser	Saft	Milch

coke	wine	beer
Cola	Wein	Bier

alcohol	cocoa	tea
Alkohol	Kakao	Tee

coffee	espresso	cappuccino
Kaffee	Espresso	Cappuccino

banana

Banane

apple

Apfel

orange

Orange

melon

Melone

lemon

Zitrone

carrot

Karotte

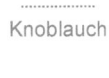

garlic

Knoblauch

bamboo

Bambus

onion

Zwiebel

mushroom

Pilz

nuts

Nüsse

noodles

Nudeln

spaghetti

Spaghetti

rice

Reis

salad

Salat

chips

Pommes frites

fried potatoes

Bratkartoffeln

pizza

Pizza

hamburger

Hamburger

sandwich

Sandwich

cutlet

Schnitzel

ham

Schinken

salami

Salami

sausage

Wurst

chicken

Huhn

roast

Braten

fish

Fisch

porridge oats

Haferflocken

muesli

Müsli

cornflakes

Cornflakes

flour

Mehl

croissant

Croissant

bread roll

Brötchen

bread

Brot

toast

Toast

biscuits

Kekse

butter

Butter

curd

Quark

cake

Kuchen

egg

Ei

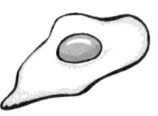

fried egg

Spiegelei

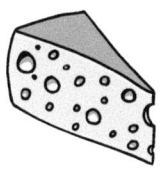

cheese

Käse

ice cream

Eiscreme

sugar

Zucker

honey

Honig

jam

Marmelade

chocolate spread

Nougat-Creme

curry

Curry

goat	cow	calf
Ziege	Kuh	Kalb

pig	piglet	bull
Schwein	Ferkel	Bulle

goose

Gans

duck

Ente

chick

Küken

hen

Huhn

cock

Hahn

rat

Ratte

cat

Katze

mouse

Maus

ox

Ochse

dog

Hund

doghouse

Hundehütte

garden hose

Gartenschlauch

watering can

Gießkanne

scythe

Sense

plough

Pflug

sickle

Sichel

hoe

Hacke

pitchfork

Mistgabel

axe

Axt

wheelbarrow

Schubkarre

trough

Trog

milk can

Milchkanne

sack

Sack

fence

Zaun

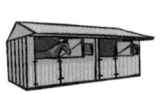

stable

Stall

greenhouse

Treibhaus

soil

Boden

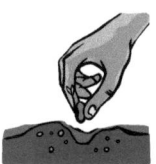

seed

Saat

fertilizer

Dünger

combine harvester

Mähdrescher

harvest

ernten

harvest

Ernte

yams

Yamswurzel

wheat

Weizen

soy

Soja

potato

Kartoffel

corn

Mais

rapeseed

Raps

fruit tree

Obstbaum

cassava

Maniok

cereals

Getreide

house
Haus

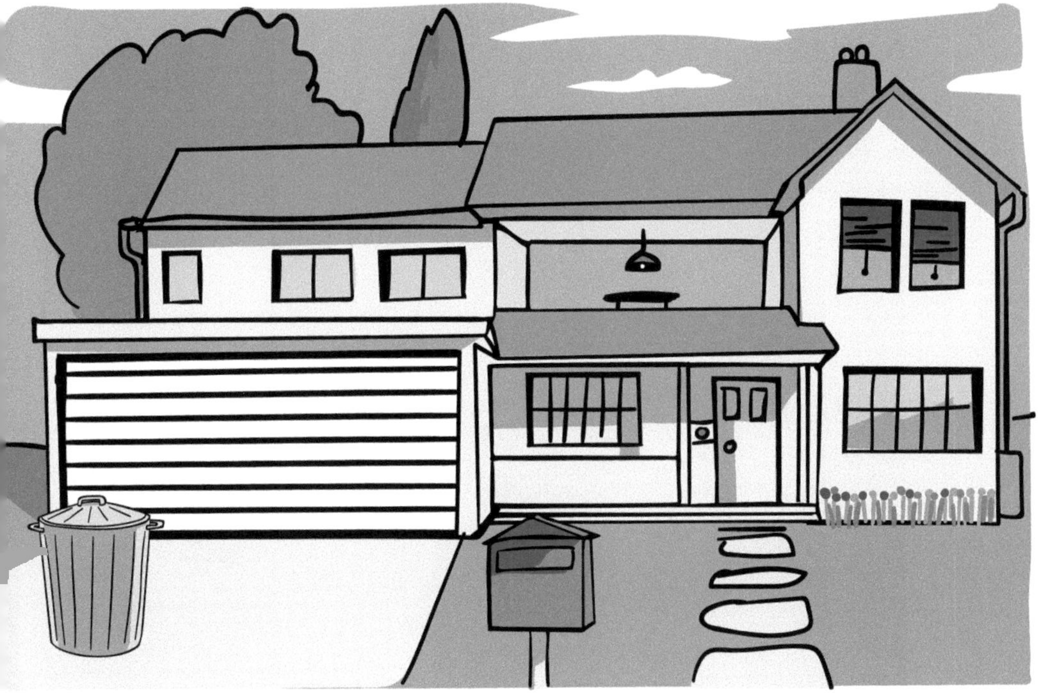

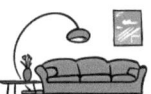

living room
Wohnzimmer

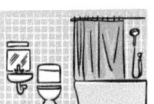

bathroom
Badezimmer

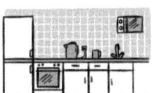

kitchen
Küche

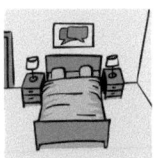

bedroom
Schlafzimmer

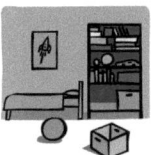

child's room
Kinderzimmer

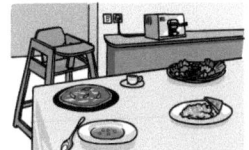

dining room
Esszimmer

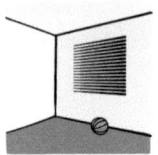

floor

Boden

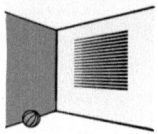

wall

Wand

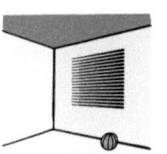

ceiling

Decke

cellar

Keller

sauna

Sauna

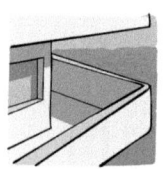

balcony

Balkon

terrace

Terrasse

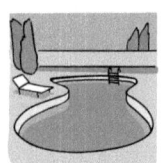

pool

Schwimmbad

lawn mower

Rasenmäher

sheet

Bettbezug

bedspread

Bettdecke

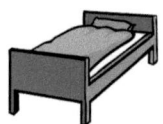

bed

Bett

broom

Besen

bucket

Eimer

switch

Schalter

carpet

Teppich

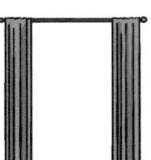

curtain

Vorhang

table

Tisch

chair

Stuhl

rocking chair

Schaukelstuhl

armchair

Sessel

book

Buch

blanket

Decke

decoration

Dekoration

firewood

Feuerholz

film

Film

hi-fi equipment

Stereoanlage

key

Schlüssel

newspaper

Zeitung

painting

Gemälde

poster

Poster

radio

Radio

notepad

Notizblock

hoover

Staubsauger

cactus

Kaktus

candle

Kerze

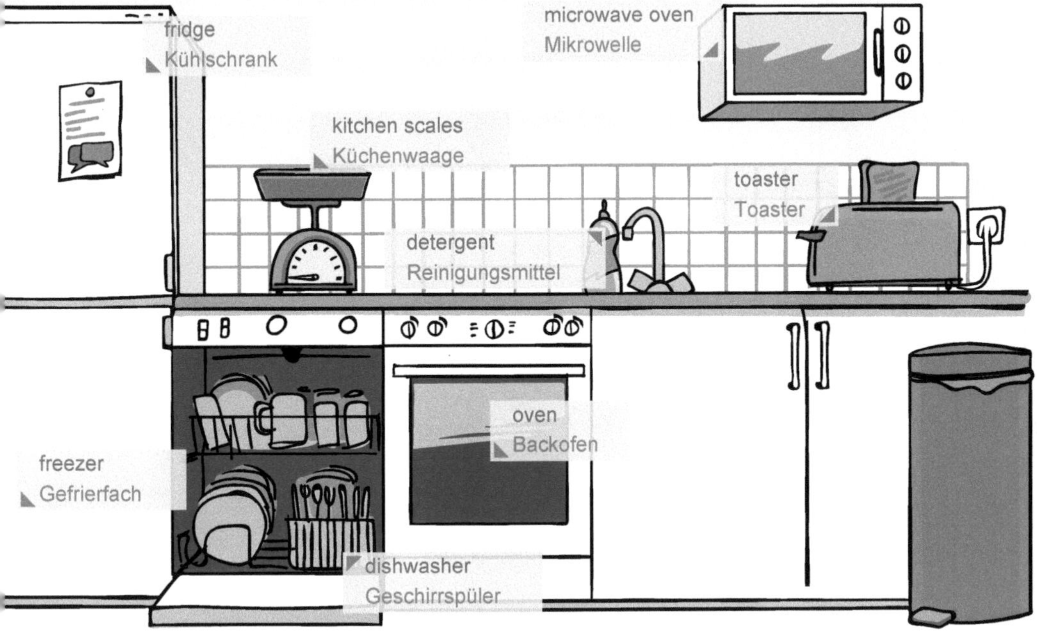

fridge
Kühlschrank

microwave oven
Mikrowelle

kitchen scales
Küchenwaage

toaster
Toaster

detergent
Reinigungsmittel

oven
Backofen

freezer
Gefrierfach

dishwasher
Geschirrspüler

cooker

Herd

pot

Topf

cast-iron pot

Eisentopf

wok / kadai

Wok / Kadai

pan

Pfanne

kettle

Wasserkocher

steamer
Dampfgarer

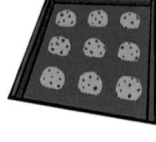

baking tray
Backblech

crockery
Geschirr

mug
Becher

bowl
Schale

chopsticks
Essstäbchen

ladle
Suppenkelle

spatula
Pfannenwender

whisk
Schneebesen

strainer
Kochsieb

sieve
Sieb

grater
Reibe

mortar
Mörser

barbecue
Grill

open fire
Feuerstelle

kitchen - Küche

chopping board

Schneidebrett

rolling pin

Nudelholz

corkscrew

Korkenzieher

can

Dose

can opener

Dosenöffner

pot holder

Topflappen

sink

Waschbecken

brush

Bürste

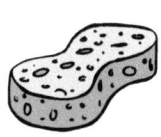

sponge

Schwamm

blender

Mixer

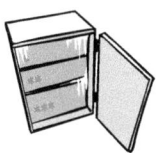

deep freezer

Gefriertruhe

baby bottle

Babyflasche

tap

Wasserhahn

kitchen - Küche

bathroom
Badezimmer

heating
Heizung
towel
Handtuch
shower
Dusche
shower curtain
Duschvorhang
bubble bath
Schaumbad
bathtub
Badewanne
glass
Glas
washing machine
Waschmaschine
tap
Wasserhahn
tiles
Fliesen
potty
Töpfchen
sink
Waschbecken

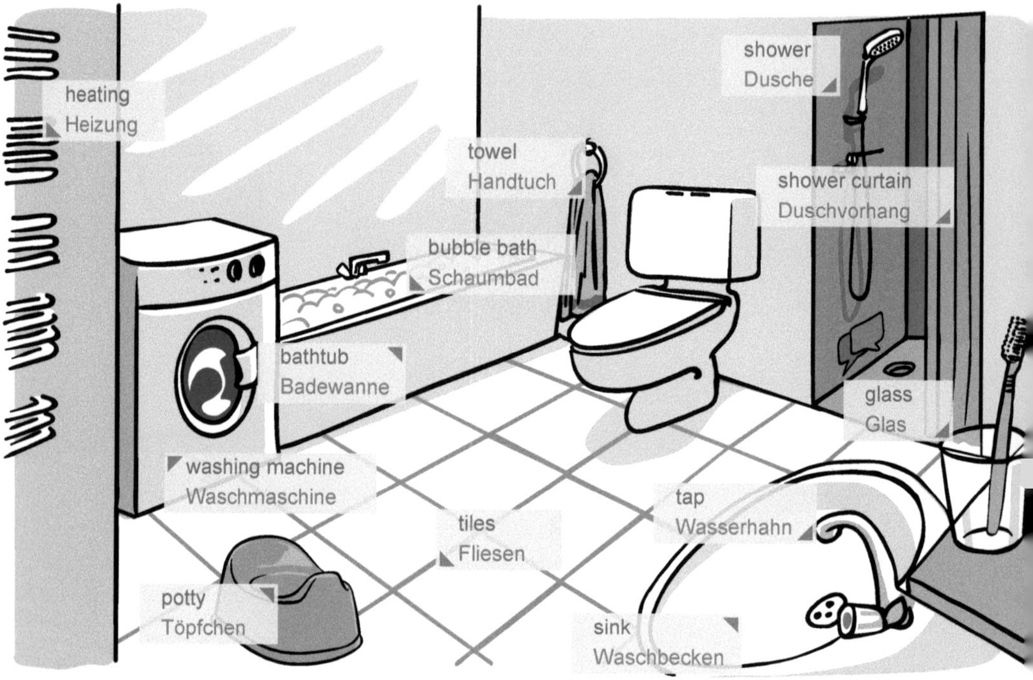

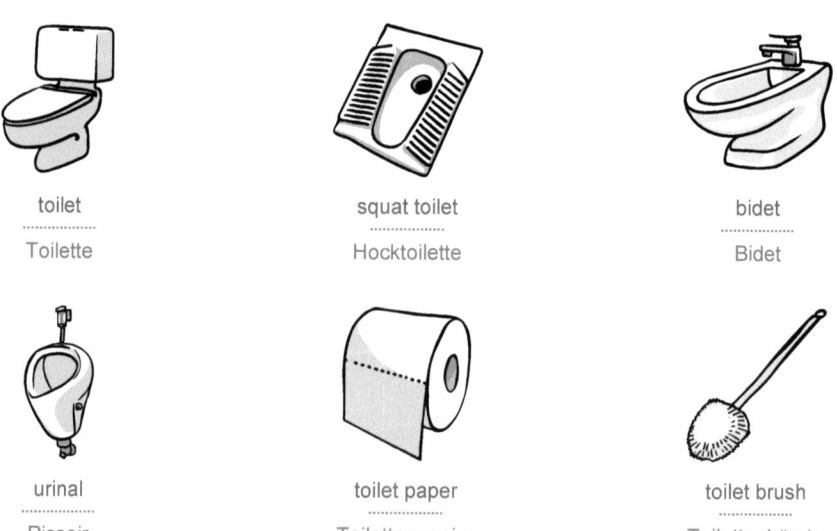

toilet
Toilette

squat toilet
Hocktoilette

bidet
Bidet

urinal
Pissoir

toilet paper
Toilettenpapier

toilet brush
Toilettenbürste

toothbrush

Zahnbürste

toothpaste

Zahnpasta

dental floss

Zahnseide

wash

waschen

handheld shower

Handbrause

douche

Intimdusche

basin

Waschschüssel

back brush

Rückenbürste

soap

Seife

shower gel

Duschgel

shampoo

Shampoo

flannel

Waschlappen

drain

Abfluss

cream

Creme

deodorant

Deodorant

mirror

Spiegel

hand mirror

Kosmetikspiegel

razor

Rasierer

shaving foam

Rasierschaum

aftershave

Rasierwasser

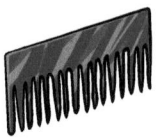

comb

Kamm

brush

Bürste

hair dryer

Föhn

hairspray

Haarspray

makeup

Makeup

lipstick

Lippenstift

nail varnish

Nagellack

cotton wool

Watte

nail scissors

Nagelschere

perfume

Parfum

washbag
Kulturbeutel

stool
Hocker

weighing scale
Waage

bathrobe
Bademantel

rubber gloves
Gummihandschuhe

tampon
Tampon

sanitary towel
Damenbinde

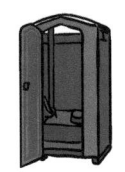

chemical toilet
Chemietoilette

child's room
Kinderzimmer

alarm clock
Wecker
cuddly toy
Kuscheltier
toy car
Spielzeugauto
rattle
Rassel
doll's house
Puppenhaus
present
Geschenk

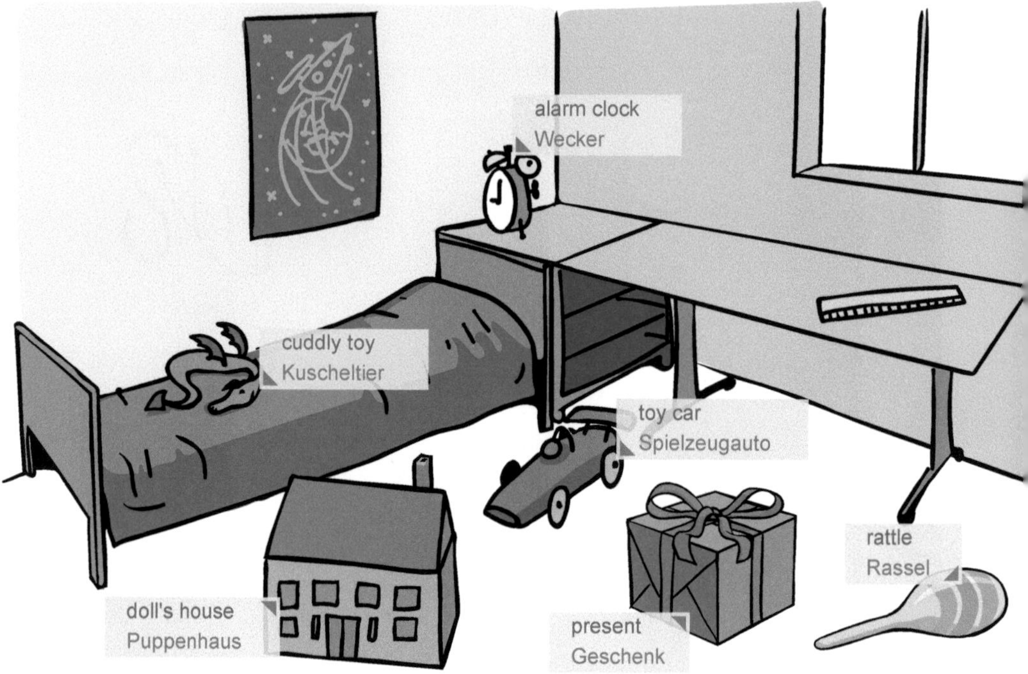

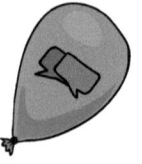

balloon

Ballon

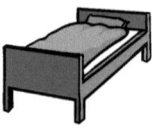

bed

Bett

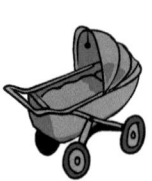

pram

Kinderwagen

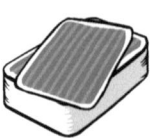

deck of cards

Kartenspiel

jigsaw

Puzzle

SUPER
MEGA

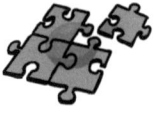

comic

Comic

lego bricks

Legosteine

building blocks

Bausteine

action figure

Action Figur

babygrow

Strampelanzug

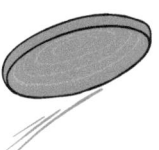

frisbee

Frisbee

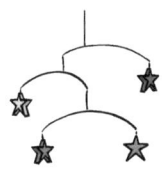

mobile

Mobile

board game

Brettspiel

dice

Würfel

model train set

Modelleisenbahn

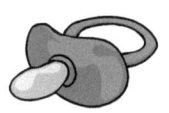

dummy

Schnuller

party

Party

picture book

Bilderbuch

ball

Ball

doll

Puppe

play

spielen

sandpit

Sandkasten

swing

Schaukel

toys

Spielzeug

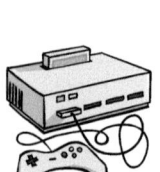

video game console

Spielkonsole

tricycle

Dreirad

teddy bear

Teddy

wardrobe

Kleiderschrank

clothing
Kleidung

socks

Socken

stockings

Strümpfe

tights

Strumpfhose

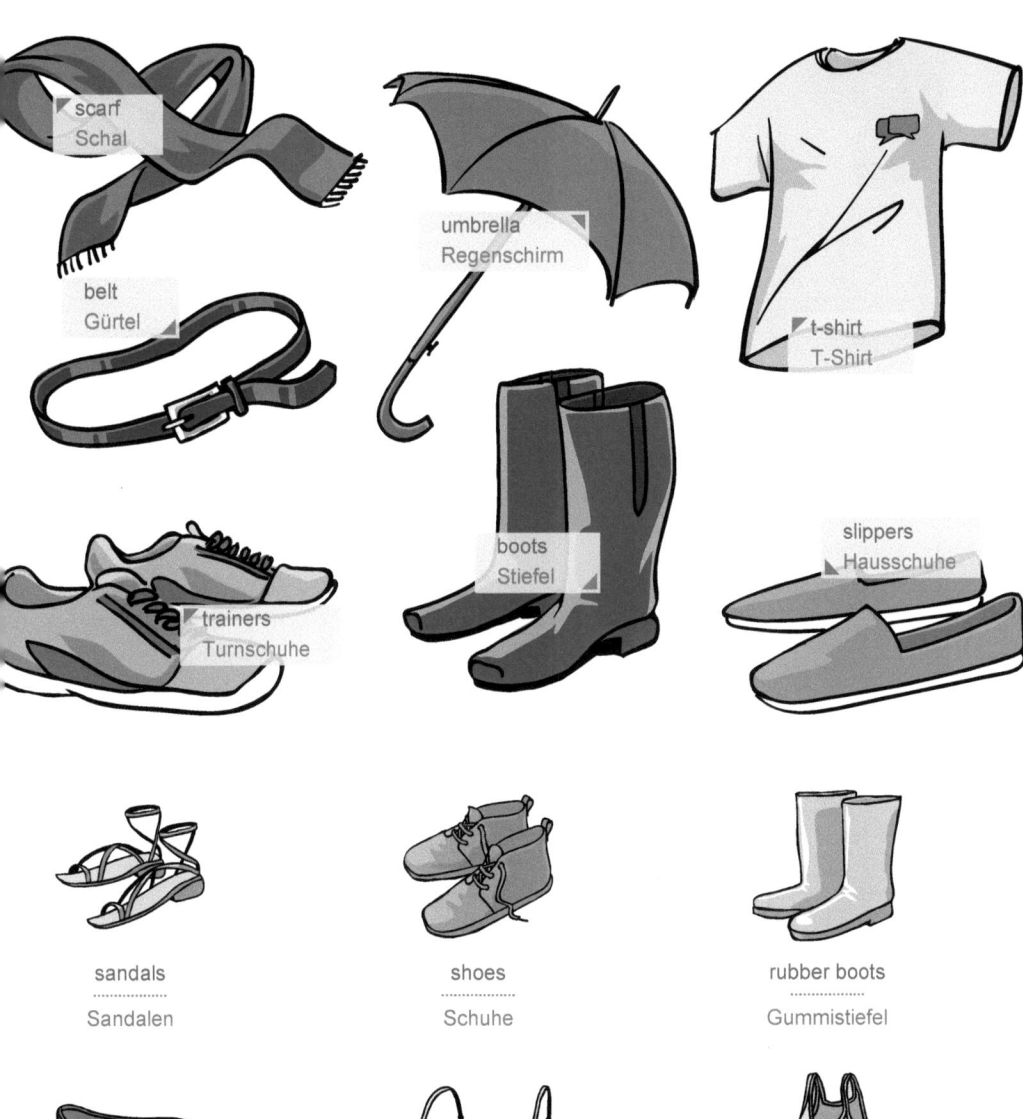

scarf
Schal

belt
Gürtel

umbrella
Regenschirm

t-shirt
T-Shirt

trainers
Turnschuhe

boots
Stiefel

slippers
Hausschuhe

sandals
Sandalen

shoes
Schuhe

rubber boots
Gummistiefel

underpants
Unterhose

bra
Büstenhalter

vest
Unterhemd

clothing - Kleidung

body

Body

trousers

Hose

jeans

Jeans

skirt

Rock

blouse

Bluse

shirt

Hemd

pullover

Pullover

hoodie

Kapuzenpullover

blazer

Blazer

jacket

Jacke

coat

Mantel

raincoat

Regenmantel

costume

Kostüm

dress

Kleid

wedding dress

Hochzeitskleid

suit

Anzug

nightgown

Nachthemd

pyjamas

Schlafanzug

sari

Sari

headscarf

Kopftuch

turban

Turban

burqa

Burka

kaftan

Kaftan

abaya

Abaya

swimsuit

Badeanzug

trunks

Badehose

shorts

Kurze Hose

tracksuit

Trainingsanzug

apron

Schürze

gloves

Handschuhe

button

Knopf

glasses

Brille

bracelet

Armband

necklace

Halskette

ring

Ring

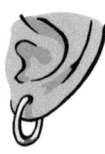

earring

Ohrring

cap

Mütze

coat hanger

Kleiderbügel

hat

Hut

tie

Krawatte

zip

Reißverschluss

helmet

Helm

braces

Hosenträger

school uniform

Schuluniform

uniform

Uniform

bib
Lätzchen

dummy
Schnuller

nappy
Windel

office
Büro

server
Server

filing cabinet
Aktenschrank

printer
Drucker

monitor
Monitor

paper
Papier

mouse
Maus

desk
Schreibtisch

folder
Ordner

keyboard
Tastatur

waste-paper basket
Papierkorb

chair
Stuhl

computer
Computer

coffee mug
Kaffeebecher

calculator
Taschenrechner

internet
Internet

laptop
Laptop

letter
Brief

message
Nachricht

mobile
Handy

network
Netzwerk

photocopier
Kopierer

software
Software

telephone
Telefon

plug socket
Steckdose

fax machine
Fax

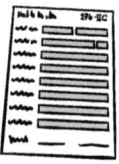

form
Formular

document
Dokument

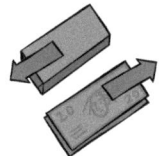

buy

kaufen

pay

bezahlen

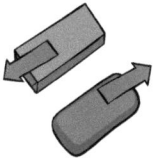

trade

handeln

money

Geld

 USD

dollar

Dollar

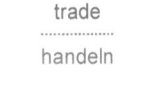 EUR

euro

Euro

 JPY

yen

Yen

 RUB

rouble

Rubel

 CHF

Swiss franc

Franken

 CNY

renminbi yuan

Renminbi Yuan

 INR

rupee

Rupie

cashpoint

Geldautomat

bureau de change

Wechselstube

gold

Gold

silver

Silber

oil

Öl

energy

Energie

price

Preis

contract

Vertrag

tax

Steuer

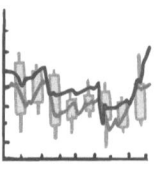

stock

Aktie

work

arbeiten

employee

Angestellter

employer

Arbeitgeber

factory

Fabrik

shop

Geschäft

economy - Wirtschaft

occupations
Berufe

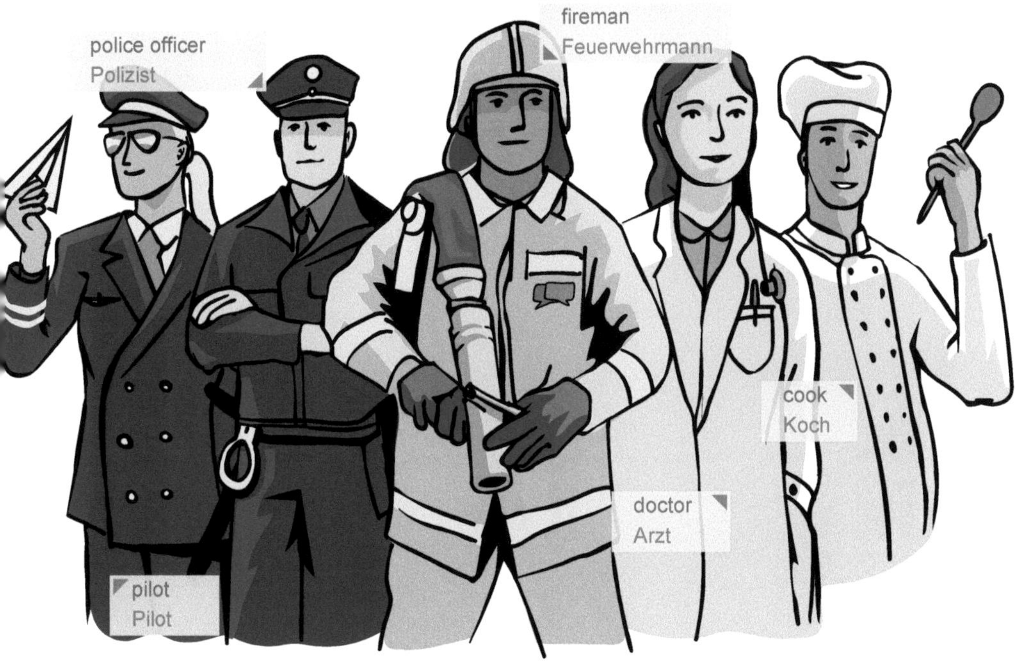
police officer
Polizist
fireman
Feuerwehrmann
cook
Koch
doctor
Arzt
pilot
Pilot

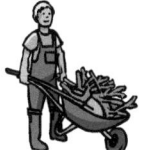

gardener

Gärtner

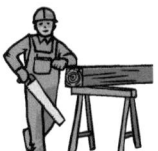

carpenter

Tischler

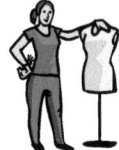

seamstress

Näherin

judge

Richter

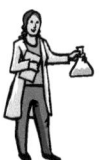

chemist

Chemiker

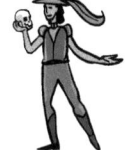

actor

Schauspieler

bus driver

Busfahrer

taxi driver

Taxifahrer

fisherman

Fischer

cleaning lady

Putzfrau

roofer

Dachdecker

waiter

Kellner

hunter

Jäger

painter

Maler

baker

Bäcker

electrician

Elektriker

builder

Bauarbeiter

engineer

Ingenieur

butcher

Schlachter

plumber

Klempner

postman

Postbote

soldier

Soldat

architect

Architekt

cashier

Kassierer

florist

Florist

hairdresser

Friseur

conductor

Schaffner

mechanic

Mechaniker

captain

Kapitän

dentist

Zahnarzt

scientist

Wissenschaftler

rabbi

Rabbi

imam

Imam

monk

Mönch

clergyman

Geistlicher

tools
Werkzeuge

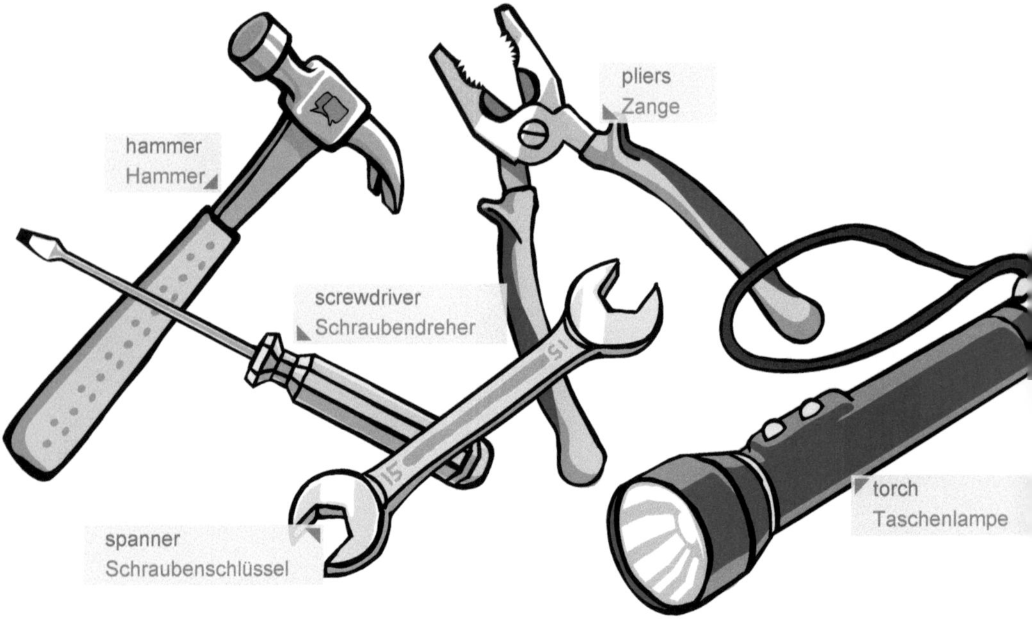

pliers
Zange
hammer
Hammer
screwdriver
Schraubendreher
spanner
Schraubenschlüssel
torch
Taschenlampe

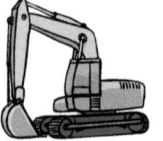

digger

Bagger

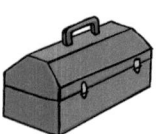

toolbox

Werkzeugkasten

ladder

Leiter

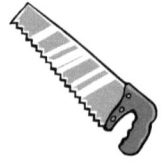

saw

Säge

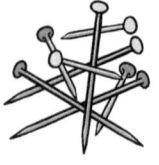

nails

Nägel

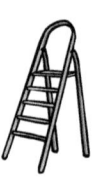

drill

Bohrer

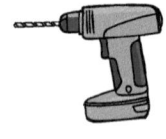

repair
reparieren

shovel
Schaufel

Damn!
Mist!

dustpan
Kehrblech

paint pot
Farbtopf

screws
Schrauben

musical instruments
Musikinstrumente

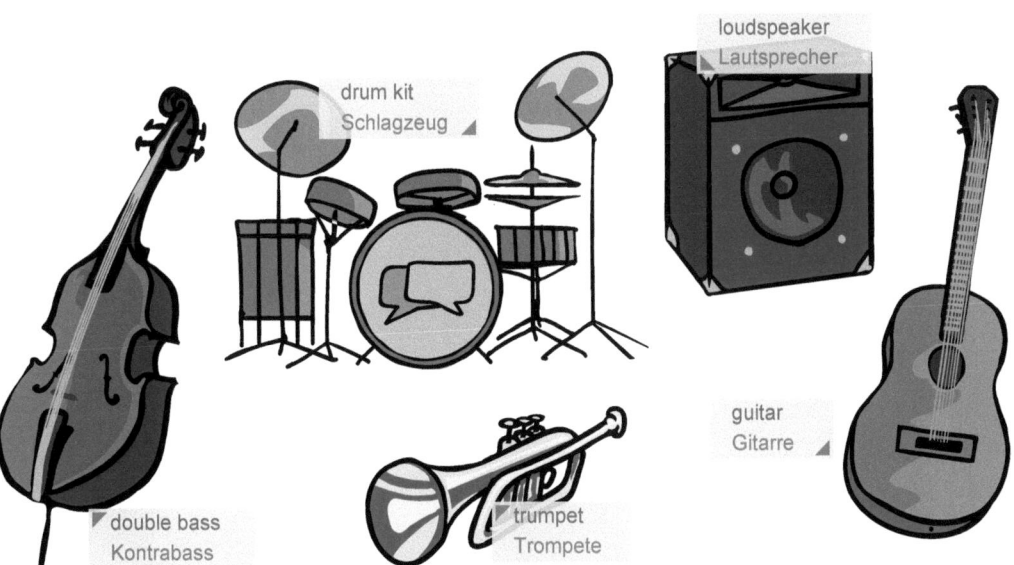

drum kit
Schlagzeug

loudspeaker
Lautsprecher

guitar
Gitarre

double bass
Kontrabass

trumpet
Trompete

piano

Klavier

violin

Violine

bass

Bass

timpani

Pauke

drums

Trommeln

keyboard

Keyboard

saxophone

Saxophon

flute

Flöte

microphone

Mikrofon

zoo
Zoo

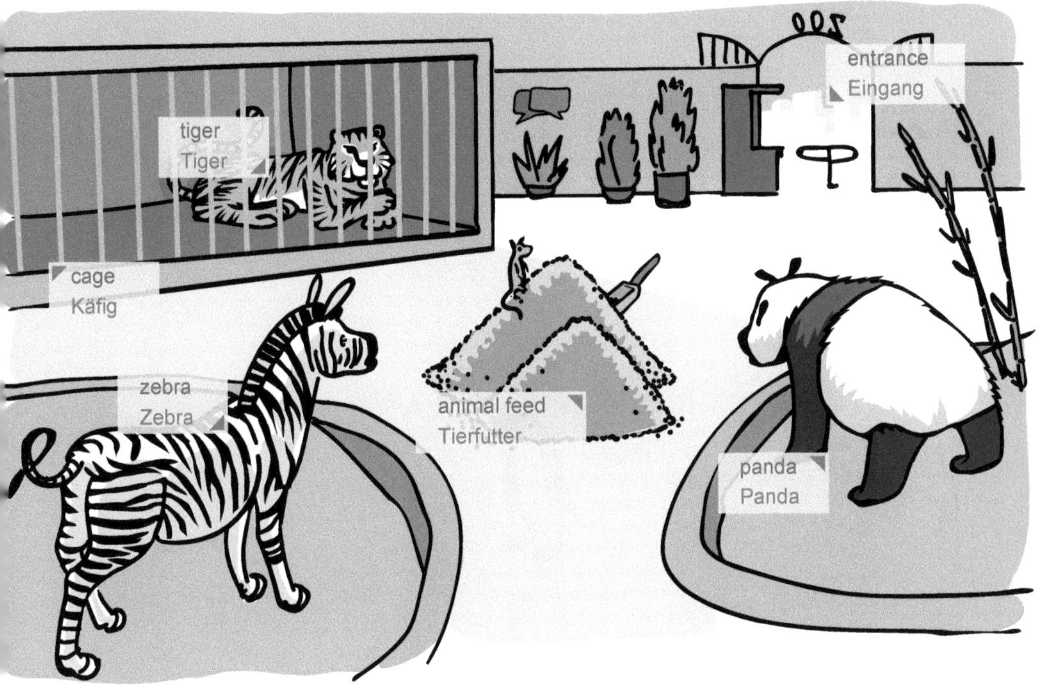
zoo
entrance
Eingang
tiger
Tiger
cage
Käfig
zebra
Zebra
animal feed
Tierfutter
panda
Panda

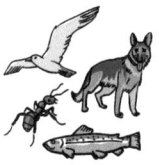

animals

Tiere

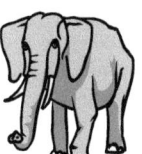

elephant

Elefant

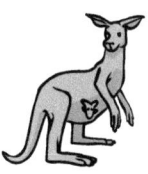

kangaroo

Känguru

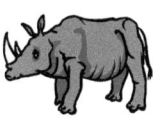

rhino

Nashorn

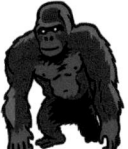

gorilla

Gorilla

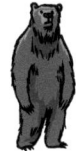

bear

Bär

camel

Kamel

ostrich

Strauß

lion

Löwe

monkey

Affe

flamingo

Flamingo

parrot

Papagei

polar bear

Eisbär

penguin

Pinguin

shark

Hai

peacock

Pfau

snake

Schlange

crocodile

Krokodil

zookeeper

Zoowärter

seal

Robbe

jaguar

Jaguar

pony

Pony

leopard

Leopard

hippo

Nilpferd

giraffe

Giraffe

eagle

Adler

boar

Wildschwein

fish

Fisch

turtle

Schildkröte

walrus

Walross

fox

Fuchs

gazelle

Gazelle

zoo - Zoo

American football
American Football

cycling
Radfahren

tennis
Tennis

basketball
Basketball

swimming
Schwimmen

boxing
Boxen

ice hockey
Eishockey

football
Fußball

badminton
Badminton

athletics
Leichtathletik

handball
Handball

skiing
Skilaufen

polo
Polo

activities
Aktivitäten

jump
springen
hug
umarmen
laugh
lachen
walk
gehen
sing
singen
dream
träumen
pray
beten
kiss
küssen

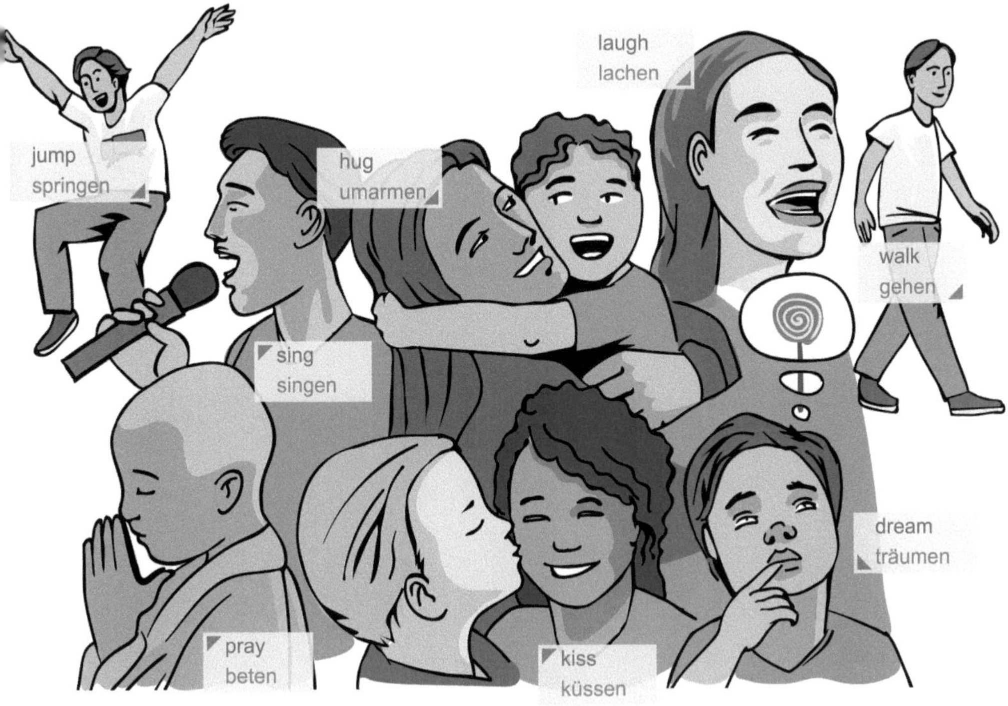

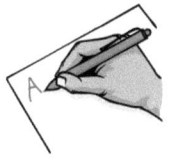

write
schreiben

draw
zeichnen

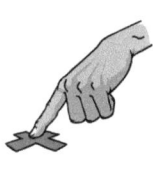

show
zeigen

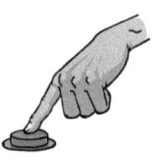

push
drücken

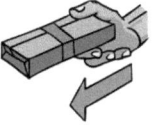

give
geben

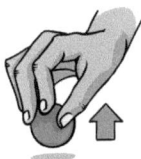

take
nehmen

have

haben

do

tun

be

sein

stand

stehen

run

laufen

pull

ziehen

throw

werfen

fall

fallen

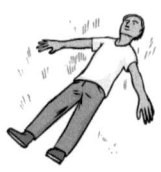

lie

liegen

wait

warten

carry

tragen

sit

sitzen

get dressed

anziehen

sleep

schlafen

wake up

aufwachen

look at

ansehen

cry

weinen

stroke

streicheln

comb

kämmen

talk

reden

understand

verstehen

ask

fragen

listen

hören

drink

trinken

eat

essen

tidy up

aufräumen

love

lieben

cook

kochen

drive

fahren

fly

fliegen

sail
segeln

calculate
rechnen

read
lesen

learn
lernen

work
arbeiten

marry
heiraten

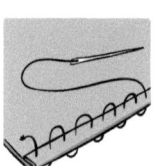

sew
nähen

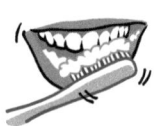

brush teeth
Zähne putzen

kill
töten

smoke
rauchen

send
senden

family
Familie

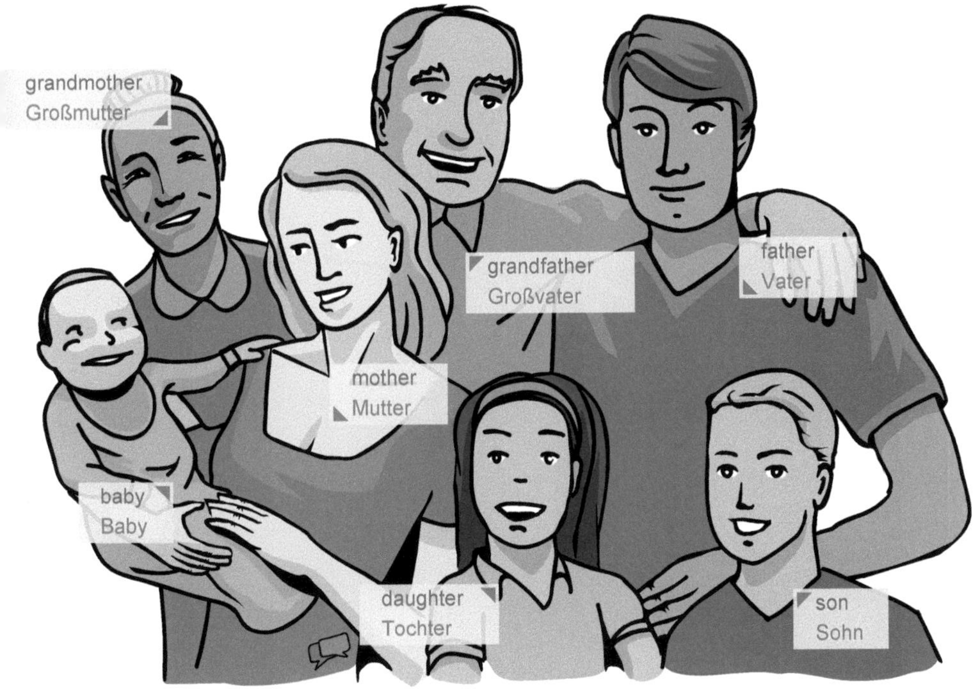

grandmother
Großmutter
grandfather
Großvater
father
Vater
mother
Mutter
baby
Baby
daughter
Tochter
son
Sohn

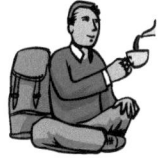

guest

Gast

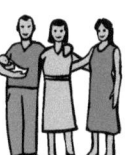

aunt

Tante

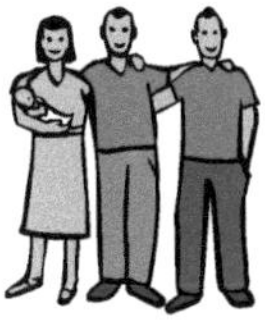

uncle

Onkel

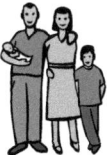

brother

Bruder

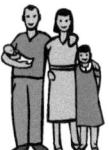

sister

Schwester

body

Körper

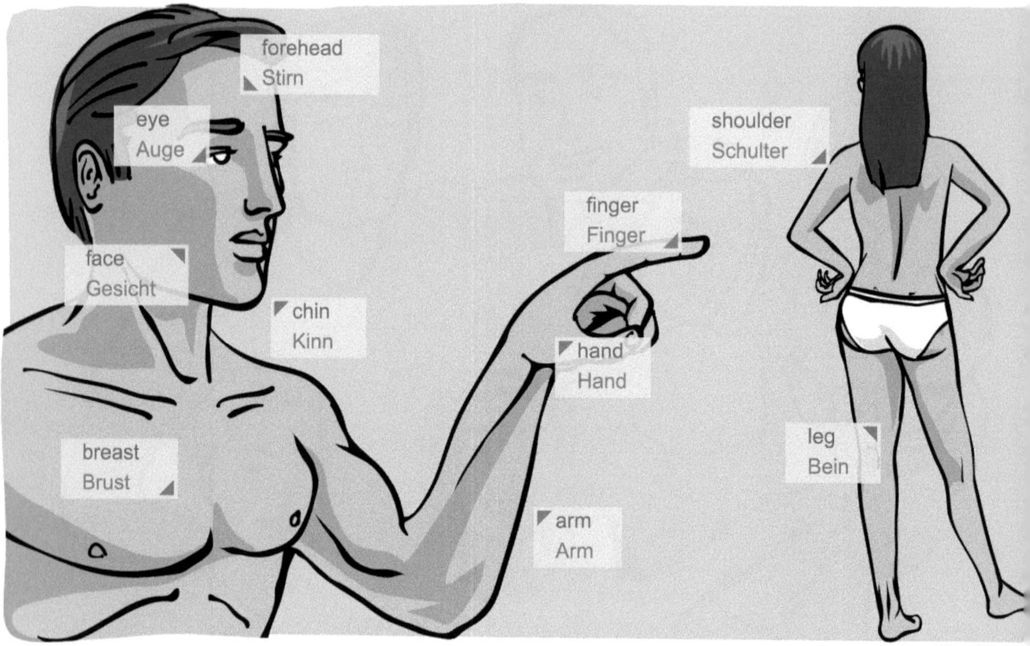

forehead
Stirn

eye
Auge

shoulder
Schulter

finger
Finger

face
Gesicht

chin
Kinn

hand
Hand

breast
Brust

leg
Bein

arm
Arm

baby

Baby

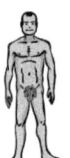

man

Mann

woman

Frau

girl

Mädchen

boy

Junge

head

Kopf

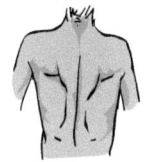

back
Rücken

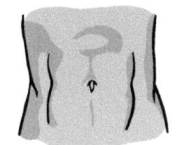

belly
Bauch

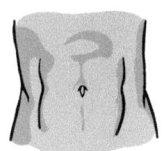

belly button
Nabel

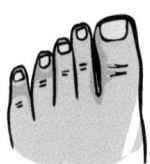

toe
Zeh

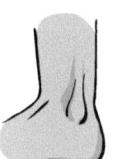

heel
Ferse

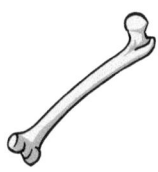

bone
Knochen

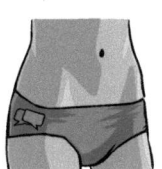

hip
Hüfte

knee
Knie

elbow
Ellenbogen

nose
Nase

bottom
Gesäß

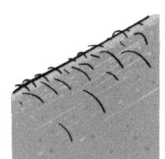

skin
Haut

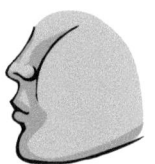

cheek
Wange

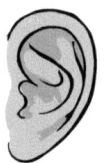

ear
Ohr

lip
Lippe

body - Körper

mouth

Mund

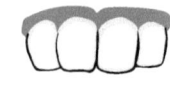

tooth

Zahn

tongue

Zunge

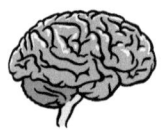

brain

Gehirn

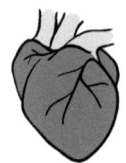

heart

Herz

muscle

Muskel

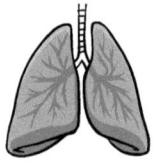

lung

Lunge

liver

Leber

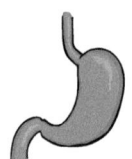

stomach

Magen

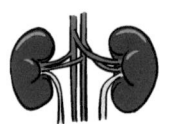

kidneys

Nieren

sex

Geschlechtsverkehr

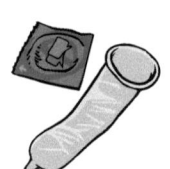

condom

Kondom

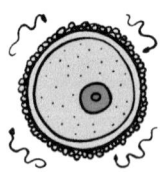

ovum

Eizelle

semen

Sperma

pregnancy

Schwangerschaft

body - Körper

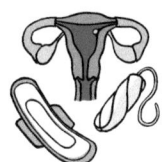

menstruation

Menstruation

vagina

Vagina

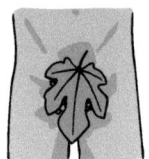

penis

Penis

eyebrow

Augenbraue

hair

Haar

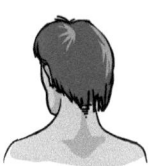

neck

Hals

hospital
Krankenhaus

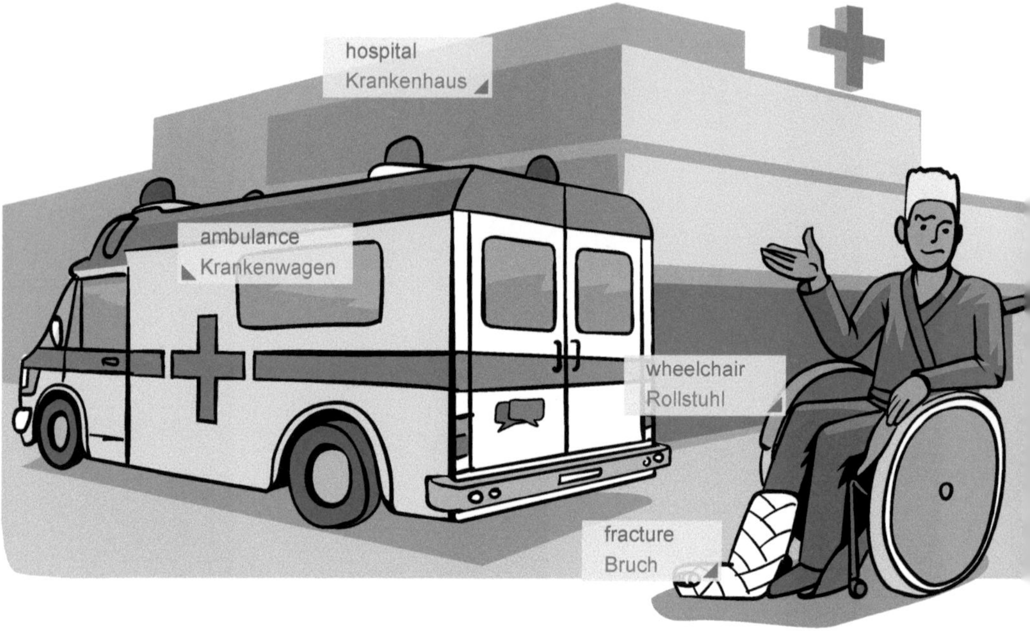

hospital
Krankenhaus
ambulance
Krankenwagen
wheelchair
Rollstuhl
fracture
Bruch

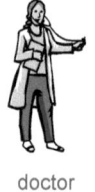

doctor
Arzt

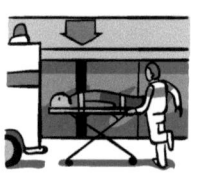

emergency room
Notaufnahme

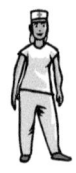

nurse
Krankenschwester

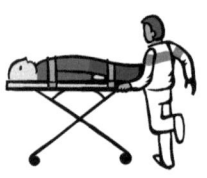

emergency
Notfall

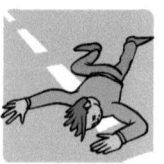

unconscious
ohnmächtig

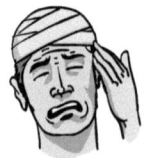

pain
Schmerz

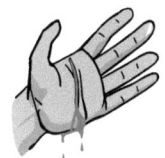

injury

Verletzung

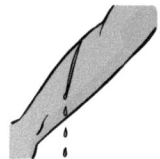

bleeding

Blutung

heart attack

Herzinfarkt

stroke

Schlaganfall

allergy

Allergie

cough

Husten

fever

Fieber

flu

Grippe

diarrhoea

Durchfall

headache

Kopfschmerzen

cancer

Krebs

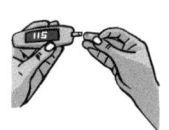

diabetes

Diabetis

surgeon

Chirurg

scalpel

Skalpell

operation

Operation

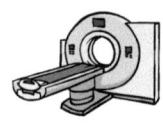

CT

CT

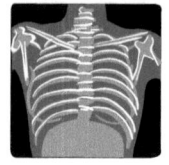

x-ray

Röntgen

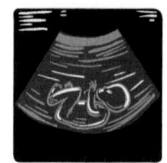

ultrasound

Ultraschall

face mask

Maske

disease

Krankheit

waiting room

Wartezimmer

crutch

Krücke

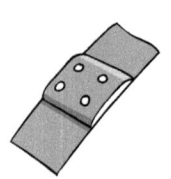

plaster

Pflaster

bandage

Verband

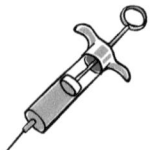

injection

Injektion

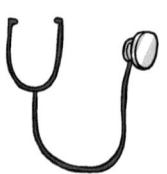

stethoscope

Stethoskop

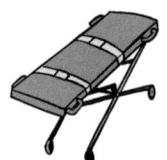

stretcher

Trage

clinical thermometer

Thermometer

birth

Geburt

overweight

Übergewicht

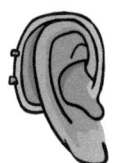

hearing aid

Hörgerät

disinfectant

Desinfektionsmittel

infection

Infektion

virus

Virus

HIV / AIDS

HIV / AIDS

medicine

Medizin

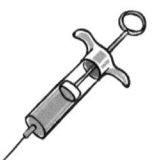

vaccination

Impfung

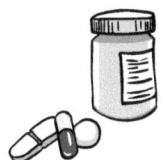

tablets

Tabletten

pill

Pille

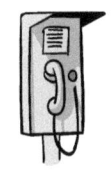

emergency call

Notruf

blood pressure monitor

Blutdruck-Messgerät

ill / healthy

krank / gesund

Help!	alarm	assault
Hilfe!	Alarm	Überfall

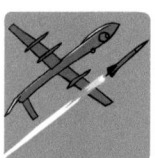

attack	danger	emergency exit
Angriff	Gefahr	Notausgang

Fire!	fire extinguisher	accident
Feuer!	Feuerlöscher	Unfall

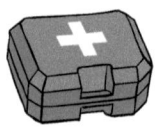

first-aid kit	SOS	police
Erste-Hilfe-Koffer	SOS	Polizei

Europe
Europa

North America
Nordamerika

South America
Südamerika

Africa
Afrika

Asia
Asien

Australia
Australien

Atlantic
Atlantik

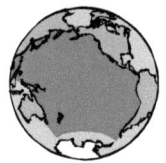

Pacific
Pazifik

Indian Ocean
Indischer Ozean

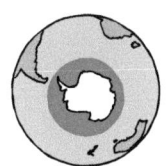

Antarctic Ocean
Antarktischer Ozean

Arctic Ocean
Arktischer Ozean

North Pole
Nordpol

South Pole
Südpol

Antarctica
Antarktis

Earth
Erde

land
Land

sea
Meer

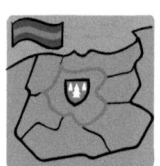

island
Insel

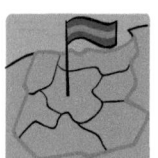

nation
Nation

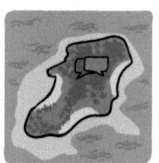

state
Staat

clock face

Zifferblatt

hour hand

Stundenzeiger

minute hand

Minutenzeiger

second hand

Sekundenzeiger

What time is it?

Wie spät ist es?

day

Tag

time

Zeit

now

jetzt

digital watch

Digitaluhr

minute

Minute

hour

Stunde

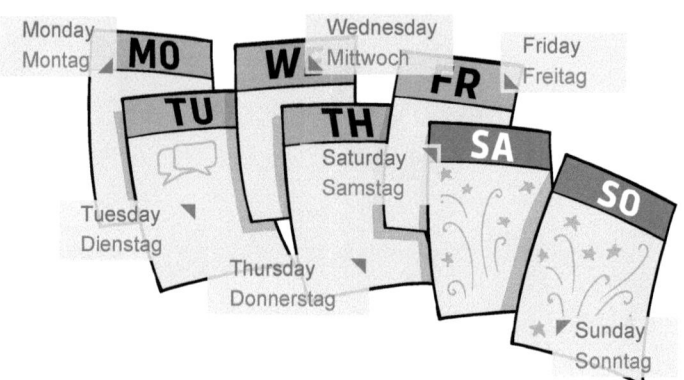

Monday / Montag
Wednesday / Mittwoch
Friday / Freitag
Tuesday / Dienstag
Saturday / Samstag
Thursday / Donnerstag
Sunday / Sonntag

yesterday

gestern

today

heute

tomorrow

morgen

morning

Morgen

noon

Mittag

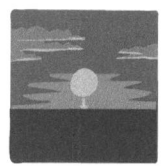

evening

Abend

MO	TU	WE	TH	FR	SA	SU
1	2	3	4	5	6	7
8	9	10	11	12	13	14
15	16	17	18	19	20	21
22	23	24	25	26	27	28
29	30	31	1	2	3	4

business days

Arbeitstage

MO	TU	WE	TH	FR	SA	SU
1	2	3	4	5	6	7
8	9	10	11	12	13	14
15	16	17	18	19	20	21
22	23	24	25	26	27	28
29	30	31	1	2	3	4

weekend

Wochenende

year
Jahr

rain
Regen
snow
Schnee
wind
Wind
spring
Frühling
autumn
Herbst
summer
Sommer
winter
Winter

4.APRIL 11°
5.APRIL 4°
6.APRIL 13°
7.APRIL 8°
8.APRIL 10°

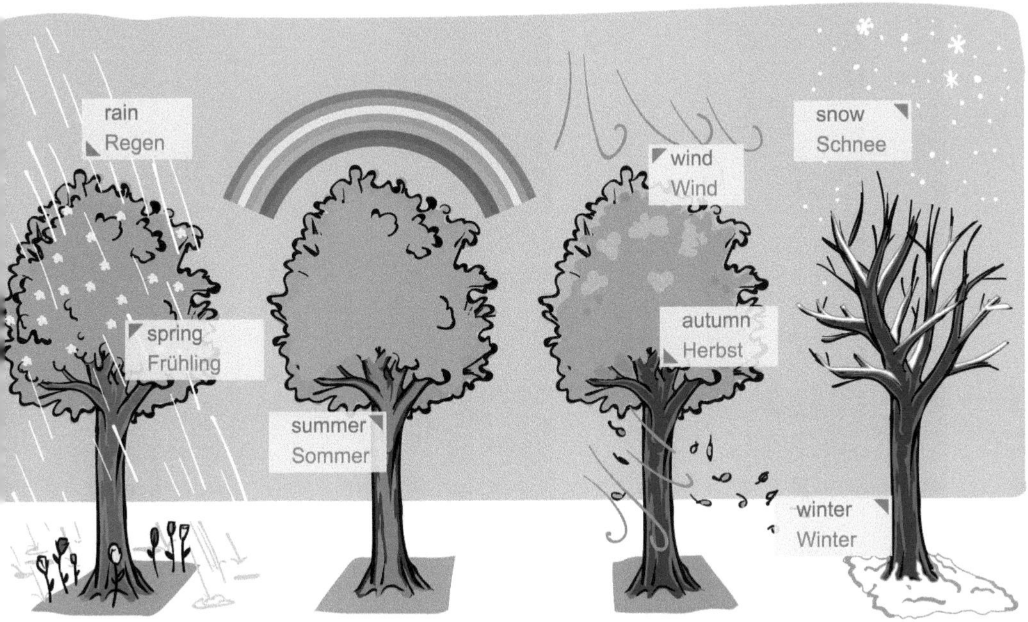

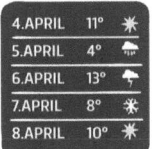

weather forecast
Wettervorhersage

F C
120 40
90 30
60 20
30 10
0 0
-30 -10
-20

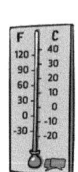

thermometer
Thermometer

sunshine
Sonnenschein

cloud
Wolke

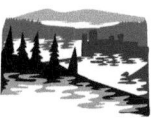

fog
Nebel

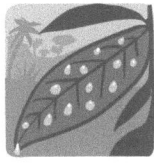

humidity
Luftfeuchtigkeit

lightning

Blitz

thunder

Donner

storm

Sturm

hail

Hagel

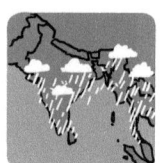

monsoon

Monsun

flood

Flut

ice

Eis

January

Januar

February

Februar

March

März

April

April

May

Mai

June

Juni

July

Juli

August

August

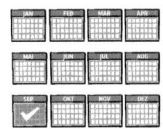

September
September

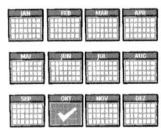

October
Oktober

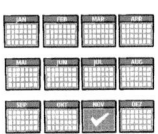

November
November

December
Dezember

shapes
Formen

circle
Kreis

square
Quadrat

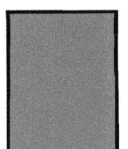

rectangle
Rechteck

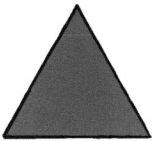

triangle
Dreieck

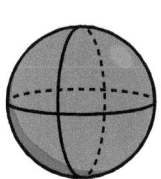

sphere
Kugel

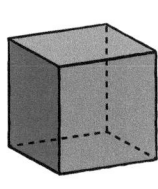

cube
Würfel

Farben

white
·······
weiß

yellow
·······
gelb

orange
·······
orange

pink
·······
pink

red
·······
rot

purple
·······
lila

blue
·······
blau

green
·······
grün

brown
·······
braun

grey
·······
grau

black
·······
schwarz

a lot / a little

viel / wenig

angry / calm

wütend / friedlich

beautiful / ugly

hübsch / hässlich

beginning / end

Anfang / Ende

big / small

groß / klein

bright / dark

hell / dunkel

brother / sister

Bruder / Schwester

clean / dirty

sauber / schmutzig

complete / incomplete

vollständig / unvollständig

day / night

Tag / Nacht

dead / alive

tot / lebendig

wide / narrow

breit / schmal

edible / inedible

genießbar / ungenießbar

evil / kind

böse / freundlich

excited / bored

aufgeregt / gelangweilt

fat / thin

dick / dünn

first / last

zuerst / zuletzt

friend / enemy

Freund / Feind

full / empty

voll / leer

hard / soft

hart / weich

heavy / light

schwer / leicht

hunger / thirst

Hunger / Durst

ill / healthy

krank / gesund

illegal / legal

illegal / legal

intelligent / stupid

intelligent / dumm

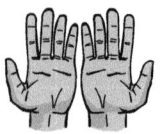

left / right

links / rechts

near / far

nah / fern

new / used
neu / gebraucht

nothing / something
nichts / etwas

old / young
alt / jung

on / off
an / aus

open / closed
offen / geschlossen

quiet / loud
leise / laut

rich / poor
reich / arm

right / wrong
richtig / falsch

rough / smooth
rau / glatt

sad / happy
traurig / glücklich

short / long
kurz / lang

slow / fast
langsam / schnell

wet / dry
nass / trocken

warm / cool
warm / kühl

war / peace
Krieg / Frieden

opposites - Gegenteile

numbers

Zahlen

0

zero

null

1

one

eins

2

two

zwei

3

three

drei

4

four

vier

5

five

fünf

6

six

sechs

7

seven

sieben

8

eight

acht

9

nine

neun

10

ten

zehn

11

eleven

elf

12	**13**	**14**
twelve	thirteen	fourteen
zwölf	dreizehn	vierzehn
15	**16**	**17**
fifteen	sixteen	seventeen
fünfzehn	sechzehn	siebzehn
18	**19**	**20**
eighteen	nineteen	twenty
achtzehn	neunzehn	zwanzig
100	**1.000**	**1.000.000**
hundred	thousand	million
hundert	tausend	million

English
Englisch

American English
Amerikanisches Englisch

Chinese Mandarin
Chinesisch Mandarin

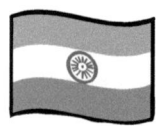

Hindi
Hindi

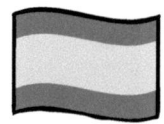

Spanish
Spanisch

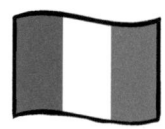

French
Französisch

Arabic
Arabisch

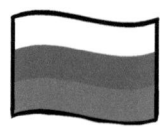

Russian
Russisch

Portuguese
Portugiesisch

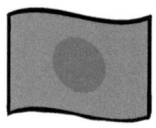

Bengali
Bengalisch

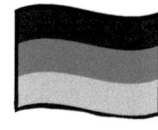

German
Deutsch

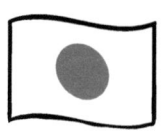

Japanese
Japanisch

I
ich

you
du

he / she / it
er / sie / es

we
wir

you
ihr

they
sie

who?
wer?

what?
was?

how?
wie?

where?
wo?

when?
wann?

name
Name

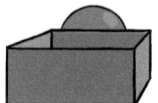

behind

hinter

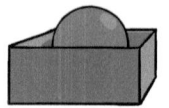

in

in

in front of

vor

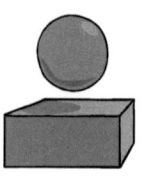

over

über

on

auf

under

unter

beside

neben

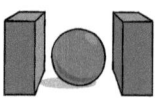

between

zwischen

place

Ort